# Anger in the Workplace

## Strategies for Professional Success

By

## Tess Palmer

# TABLE OF CONTENTS

**CHAPTER 7**
**SURVIVING A POSITIVE WORK**
**ENVIRONMENT**
THE SIGNIFICANCE OF A HAPPY
WORKPLACE
**<u>CONCLUSION</u>**

# CHAPTER 1
# UNDERSTANDING WORKPLACE ANGER

A complicated and multidimensional emotion, workplace anger can have a significant impact on people's lives and the atmosphere at work. It can come from several things, such as internal conflicts or outside pressures from work, deadlines, or coworker relationships.

## DIFFERENT TYPES OF WORKPLACE ANGER

Effective handling of anger at work requires an understanding of its various forms.

**Anger Rooted in Frustration**: This results from challenges, setbacks, or expectations not being fulfilled in work-related duties. It might be aimed against the company, oneself, or peers.

**Interpersonal Conflict-Related Anger**: Resulting from miscommunications, conflicts of interest, or disputes with coworkers or superiors. It could result from values, work methods, or communication style disparities.

**Stress-Induced Anger**: Caused by circumstances involving a lot of pressure, an overwhelming workload, or irrational expectations. Chronic rage problems might arise due to prolonged exposure to chronic stressors.

**Perceived Injustice Anger**: This is the emotion that arises when a worker believes they have been mistreated regarding assignments, promotions, or recognition. Hostility and resentment may result from this.

## EFFECTS OF ANGER AT WORK

Anger management gone wrong at work can hurt employees and the company as a whole:

**<u>Decreased Productivity</u>**: Anger impairs concentration, judgment, and ability to work through tasks effectively.

**<u>Deterioration of Working Relationships</u>**: It can cause Stress in relationships between coworkers, undermine trust, and foster an unfriendly work atmosphere.

**<u>Negative Health Consequences</u>**: Stress is linked to chronic anger and can cause various physical and mental health problems.

**<u>Decreased Job Satisfaction and Engagement</u>**: Prolonged exposure to rage can cause disengagement from the workplace and a decline in job satisfaction.

## IDENTIFYING TRIGGERS AND WARNING INDICATIONS

To effectively respond, people must recognize the distinct triggers and early indicators of anger:

**Physical Signs**: These could be clenched fists, shallow breathing, tense muscles, or elevated heart rate.

**Cognitive Signs**: Anger episodes may be preceded by racing thoughts, negative self-talk, or illogical thought patterns.

**Behavioral Signs**: These can include more overt displays of anger, including raised voices or forceful gestures, as well as passive-aggressive behavior.

People aware of these indicators can take proactive measures to control their rage and keep it from worsening.

# FOSTERING EMOTIONAL INTELLIGENCE

Understanding and controlling workplace anger requires developing emotional intelligence and self-awareness. This entails being aware of one's emotions, comprehending where they come from, and learning how to control them positively.

Gaining a firm understanding of the subtleties of workplace anger is essential to putting anger management techniques into practice and achieving success in the Office.

Let's examine workplace fury in more detail:

## ORGANIZATIONAL CULTURE'S ROLE

An organization's culture dramatically impacts how people express and control their emotions. A positive workplace culture encourages candid communication, facilitates the resolution of disputes, and gives staff members a constructive platform to express their concerns. On the other hand, suppressing emotions in a toxic or repressive culture can result in rage building up and potentially exploding in destructive ways.

## VARIATIONS IN ANGER EXPRESSION AMONG INDIVIDUALS

Individual differences in temperament, upbringing, and cultural background affect how people display anger. Some people communicate more assertively, while others might tend to bottle up their rage. To create a healthy work atmosphere that accepts a variety of approaches to emotion processing and expression, it is imperative to recognize these individual variances.

### The Anger at Work Ripple Effect

Anger in the workplace affects the whole company; it doesn't exist in a vacuum. If left unchecked, it can impair team dynamics, productivity, and general morale. It can also spread like wildfire. On the other hand, a culture of respect, empathy, and cooperation can be fostered in the workplace by skillfully controlling and transforming anger.

## How Personal and Professional Lives Intersect

It's critical to understand that feelings from one's personal life can influence one's work environment and vice versa. Relationship problems or financial strain are examples of non-job-related events that can significantly impact someone's emotional state at work. It is imperative to recognize this connection to offer comprehensive help and tools for anger management.

<u>**Cultural and Gender Aspects to Consider**</u>
How rage is perceived and displayed can be influenced by cultural norms and expectations. Furthermore, research indicates that cultural expectations frequently influence the gendered patterns of rage display. Comprehending these subtleties is vital in advancing inclusivity and circumventing preconceptions around the production of anger in professional settings.

<u>**SEEKING EXPERT ASSISTANCE**</u>
For certain people, getting help from counselors, anger management experts, or mental health specialists may be necessary to control their workplace rage. Offering tools and channels for staff to get expert assistance shows a commitment to their welfare and fosters a more welcoming and encouraging work environment.

Comprehending the complex aspects of anger in the workplace gives people and organizations the information they need to put focused anger management, conflict resolution, and professional achievement methods into practice.

# CHAPTER 2:
## THE PSYCHOLOGICAL DYNAMICS OF ANGER

It's crucial to comprehend the psychological foundations of rage to control this strong feeling on the job. This chapter explores the complex interactions between feelings, ideas, and outside circumstances that lead to the experience of rage.

## EXAMINING THE EMOTIONAL ENVIRONMENT

Anger is a complicated emotion that frequently combines with fear, sadness, disappointment, and frustration. By doing this, people can learn more about the underlying emotional terrain and the reasons behind their anger. For example, the anxiety of failing a task can intensify frustration, resulting in a powerful combination of feelings.

## Interpretations and Cognitive Assessments

People's interpretations and assessments of situations greatly impact how they feel. Anger can be exacerbated by negative cognitive patterns like personalizing or catastrophizing events. Reframing events and controlling anger productively need an awareness of and resistance to these cognitive distortions.

## Hot Buttons and Triggers

Specific circumstances or impulses bring on anger. These triggers may be pretty intimate, derived from prior encounters, or connected to certain facets of a person's line of work. Being able to recognize these triggers gives people the ability to foresee and handle potentially difficult circumstances with more awareness and control.

## Individual Variables in Fury Expression

Individual variances highly influence anger expression in temperament, personality traits, and coping techniques. While some people may be more prone to brief outbursts of rage, others may have a higher threshold for annoyance. Comprehending these individual variables facilitates customized methods for managing anger.

## Anger-Inducing Organisational Factors

Anger can be lessened or increased depending on the workplace atmosphere. Anger at work can be increased by several things, including poor communication, a lack of transparency, irrational expectations, or a blame culture. It is essential to understand these organizational dynamics to put systemic changes into place that support a more positive work environment.

## Hierarchies and Power Dynamics

Employees may become angry and frustrated with power disparities inside the company. Sentiment and helplessness can result from perceived injustices or a lack of agency in decision-making processes. Promoting a more inclusive and fair workplace requires addressing and reducing these power imbalances.

## ADAPTIVE REACTIONS AND COPING STRATEGIES

Comprehending appropriate coping strategies is essential for proficiently handling rage. We examine various adaptive strategies that enable people to manage difficult circumstances with poise and resilience, including assertive communication, mindfulness exercises, and stress-reduction methods.

People can learn a great deal about the fundamental causes of workplace anger by exploring the psychological aspects of anger.

Developing targeted methods for professional achievement and anger management starts with this insight.

# CHAPTER 3
## EFFECTIVE COMMUNICATION UNDER HIGH-STRESS CONDITIONS

Gaining proficiency in good communication is essential for controlling anger and defusing potentially explosive situations in a high-stakes job setting. Developing the abilities required to handle difficult conversations and express oneself assertively is the primary goal of this chapter.

## Finding the Balance in Assertive Communication

To convey demands and concerns while respecting the rights and boundaries of others, assertive communication is an essential skill. It entails speaking one's mind straightforwardly, sincerely, and self-assuredly without using force or inaction. The methods for finding the ideal balance between diplomacy and aggressiveness are covered in this chapter.

## Paying Attention and Reacting with Empathy

Efficient communication also requires attentive listening. Developing rapport and trust requires understanding other people's viewpoints and concerns. This chapter offers techniques for careful listening and sympathetic answers affirming coworkers' emotions and experiences.

## "I" Declarations and Nonviolent Transference of Power**

"I" statements are an effective means of communicating wants and sentiments without placing blame. This chapter explores the composition of "I" statements and presents ideas from the Nonviolent Communication (NVC) paradigm, emphasizing understanding and empathy in communication.

## STRATEGIES FOR DE-ESCALATION

Possessing a toolkit of de-escalation tactics is very helpful when tensions are high. This chapter provides valuable methods for calming tense circumstances, such as keeping a composed expression, using verbal cues to soothe feelings, and establishing a safe conversation environment.

## TECHNIQUES FOR RESOLVING CONFLICTS

In any job, conflict is unavoidable, but how it is handled can have a significant impact. Several conflict resolution techniques are covered in this chapter, such as collaborative problem-solving, mediation, and win-win negotiation. People can use these strategies to turn disagreements into chances for learning and development.

## Conscientious Interaction

Being present, conscious of one's emotions, and aware of the effects of words and body language are all components of practicing mindfulness in communication. You need to become more conscious during interactions so you can react deliberately as opposed to instinctively.

## Setting Limits and Advocating for Oneself

An essential component of assertive communication is establishing and upholding healthy boundaries. setting limits is important, as expressing them clearly and making demands known without jeopardizing one's well-being.

People may handle high-pressure situations with poise and confidence by developing their assertive communication skills and de-escalation techniques. These resources help create a more cooperative and peaceful work atmosphere and defuse tension.

## Handling Emotional Suppression in Interaction

Severe circumstances frequently elicit potent feelings. Recognizing and controlling these emotional triggers is the primary goal of this section. Deep breathing, grounding exercises, and cognitive reframing are a few strategies that can help people stay calm and coherent during heated discussions.

## Adaptive Reactions and Conflict Styles

It's important to recognize one's default conflict style, whether cooperating, compromising, accommodating, competing, or avoiding. You need to examine the advantages and disadvantages of each type and offer suggestions for when to modify and use various methods based on the circumstances.

## Fostering Cultural Intelligence in Interaction

Communication that is sensitive to cultural differences is essential in diverse workplaces. The significance of comprehending cultural conventions, values, and communication styles is covered in this section. It offers advice on promoting diversity, preventing miscommunication, and creating connections between people with different viewpoints.

## Handling Hierarchical Structures

Good communication can be challenging in companies with distinct hierarchies. This chapter provides advice on negotiating power relationships. These tactics include politely expressing problems, asking for input, and pushing for reform in a hierarchical setting.

## TECHNIQUES FOR EMOTIONAL REGULATION

Anger is one of the strong, sometimes overpowering emotions. This section presents valuable methods for controlling emotions, including journaling, progressive muscle relaxation, and mindfulness exercises. With the help of these resources, people can actively learn to control their emotions even under stressful circumstances.

### Exercises in Role-Playing and Simulation

Practice makes perfect, especially when it comes to communication abilities. To practice assertive communication, de-escalation, and conflict resolution in a safe and controlled setting, this chapter offers role-playing scenarios and simulation exercises.

### Constructive Criticism and Feedback

Giving and getting feedback is a crucial component of good communication.

This section provides instructions on how to provide feedback that is actionable, specific, and constructive. It also offers methods for applying criticism as a tool for personal development and accepting it with an open mind.

**<u>Establishing rapport and trust</u>**
Effective communication is built on trust. There are ways to establish trust, such as being dependable and honest, communicating openly, and consistently keeping your word.

Communicating effectively under duress enables people to handle challenging circumstances with professionalism and elegance. By using these techniques, people control their emotions and promote an environment at work where communication is courteous, open, and cooperative.

# CHAPTER 4
## EMOTIONAL INTELLIGENCE AND ANGER MANAGEMENT

To effectively manage emotions, especially anger, in professional contexts, emotional intelligence (EI) is a critical skill set. This chapter explores the elements of emotional intelligence (EI) and how to use them to manage relationships and obstacles at work.

RecognizingEmotional Intelligence

## FOUR MAIN ELEMENTS MAKE UP EMOTIONAL INTELLIGENCE:

**Self-awareness**: Acknowledging and comprehending one's feelings, including the patterns and triggers connected to rage.

**Self-regulation**: The capacity to restrain and control one's emotions, especially under duress.

**Empathy**: Responding sensitively while comprehending and respecting the feelings and viewpoints of others.

**Social skills**: The ability to successfully negotiate social situations, form bonds with others, and communicate.

## DEVELOPING EMOTIONAL INTELLIGENCE

One of the first steps towards controlling anger is increasing self-awareness. To assist people in identifying the early indicators of anger and comprehending the underlying feelings, this section offers activities and approaches to increase emotional awareness.

### Fostering Self-Control

Self-regulation allows people to control their emotions and stop them from spiraling out of control and into harmful behavior. This provides valuable techniques to improve self-regulation in work environments, including deep breathing exercises, mindfulness techniques, and cognitive reframing.

## Empathy Practises in the Workplace

Empathy is an effective strategy for resolving disputes and fostering long-lasting business partnerships. This section offers advice on how to show empathy, take a perspective, and actively listen—even under challenging circumstances.

## USING EMOTIONAL INTELLIGENCE TO RESOLVE CONFLICT

In particular, emotional intelligence is very important for resolving conflicts.
This looks at how social skills, self-control, empathy, and self-awareness can be used to navigate and settle disputes at work politely and productively.

## Identifying and Handling Emotional Cues

People with emotional intelligence are better able to recognize and deal with emotional cues. People can use focused techniques to control their emotional reactions by being aware of the particular encounters, events, or scenarios that make them angry.

## Fostering and Preserving Positive Connections

Effective communication, mutual respect, and trust are the foundation of strong working partnerships. This section offers insights into the role that emotional intelligence plays in establishing and preserving healthy, fruitful relationships with coworkers, managers, and clients.

## Using Social Intelligence to Strengthen Leadership

Leading effectively is characterized by emotional intelligence. This covers the application of emotional intelligence (EI) principles by leaders to encourage and inspire their colleagues, deal with difficult circumstances, and create a welcoming and productive work atmosphere.

Enhancing emotional awareness, self-regulation, and empathy helps people control their anger and deal with obstacles at work in a classy and professional manner. Applying emotional intelligence not only promotes a more peaceful workplace but also advances both individual and professional development.

# CHAPTER 5
## CONSTRUCTIVE CONFLICT RESOLUTION

Professional life will inevitably involve conflict. A vital talent for preserving a positive work atmosphere is the ability to resolve issues amicably and respectfully. We will examine methods and approaches for handling disputes and coming to amicable agreements.

## KNOWING WHAT KIND OF CONFLICT THERE IS

Before learning about conflict resolution strategies, it's critical to realize that conflict results from divergent needs, goals, and views. The first step to handling conflict healthily is realizing that it is an inevitable component of any dynamic workplace.

## Empathetic Communication and Active Listening

Constructive conflict resolution is based on active listening.

Guidelines for attentive listening are provided in this section to help parties better grasp one another's perspectives. Empathetic communication also promotes an atmosphere of respect and understanding between people.

## Making Sense of Things and Determining Interests

It's critical to define the precise problems at hand and determine the underlying interests of each party to resolve disagreements amicably. This provides methods for identifying the central issues and motivations behind the conflict.

## Coming Up with Innovative Solutions

It takes creativity to solve problems and come up with solutions that benefit both parties. This presents methods for brainstorming ideas and working together to create a wider range of possibilities and creative solutions.

## Strategies for Mediation

Mediation can be an effective strategy in cases where disputes intensify or become very entrenched. This chapter describes several mediation strategies, such as the use of an impartial third-party mediator to let parties communicate freely and work towards a settlement.

## TECHNIQUES FOR BARGAINING

One essential component of resolving conflicts is negotiation. Effective negotiating techniques are covered in this section. These include establishing clear goals, comprehending each party's best alternative to a negotiated agreement (BATNA), and looking for win-win alternatives.

## Resolving Conflict and Being Assertive

Since it enables people to voice their demands and concerns while respecting the rights and viewpoints of others, assertiveness is crucial in conflict resolution. This examines assertive communication strategies that enable people to stand up for themselves.

## Handling Conflict-Related Emotions
Conflict resolution may be hampered by the strong emotions involved. This provides strategies for handling emotions, such as self-regulation exercises, mindfulness exercises, and methods for maintaining composure.

## Agreement, Implementation, and Aftercare
The first step in resolving a problem is merely that. The significance of recording agreements and putting in place a follow-up procedure to guarantee that the decided-upon solutions are carried out successfully is covered in this chapter.

By using these methods and approaches, people can turn disagreements from sources of Stress to chances for development, better relationships, and enhanced communication at work. Finding solutions is just one aspect of constructive conflict resolution; another is fostering a climate of mutual respect and cooperation in the workplace.

# CHAPTER 6:
## MANAGING STRESS AND TAKING CARE OF ONESELF

Stress management and making self-care a priority is crucial for preserving mental and emotional health in today's hectic work situations. To lower stress levels and avoid building up resentment, this emphasizes the use of self-care techniques. It also stresses the significance of striking a balance between one's personal and professional obligations.

## Understanding Stress's Effects

The first step to effective stress management is realizing how Stress affects one's mental, emotional, and physical well-being. This emphasizes the significance of proactive self-care and the range of manifestations that chronic Stress can take.

## Putting Self-Care Practises in Place

A variety of activities that support one's mental, emotional, and physical health are included in self-care.

This offers helpful advice on creating self-care regimens that include regular exercise, mindfulness training, getting enough sleep, and maintaining a balanced diet.

## Stress Management and Mindfulness

A useful strategy for controlling Stress and avoiding the accumulation of rage is mindfulness. This presents mindfulness practices that encourage relaxation and present-moment awareness, such as deep breathing exercises, body scans, and meditation.

## Determining Limitations for Work-Life Harmony

To avoid burnout and preserve well-being, it's essential to set clear boundaries between work and personal obligations.

provides time management ideas and assertive communication tactics for establishing and upholding appropriate boundaries.

## Using Techniques for Relaxation

Stress levels can be considerably lowered by incorporating relaxation techniques into daily activities. With a variety of techniques to help people relax and de-stress, this area covers progressive muscle relaxation, guided imagery, and aromatherapy.

## Fostering Passions and Interests

One of the most important aspects of self-care is doing things that make you happy and fulfilled. To promote creativity, relaxation, and renewal, encourages people to discover and pursue interests and hobbies outside of the workplace.

## Seeking Online Assistance

Emotional health depends on maintaining solid social ties. The significance of asking friends, family, and coworkers for help is emphasized in this section. It offers pointers on how to establish a support system and communicate effectively.

## Prioritization and Time Management

Managing your time well is essential to strike a balance between your personal and professional obligations. This chapter provides helpful advice on how to prioritize chores, set realistic objectives, and maximize productivity so that you have time for self-care.

## Examining and Modifying Practises for Self-Care

Self-care is an evolving process that can call for modifications in the future. This part encourages people to evaluate their self-care regimens regularly, pinpoint areas for development, and modify techniques to accommodate evolving requirements and situations.

By putting these self-care techniques into practice and placing a high value on their health, people may effectively manage Stress, stop anger from building up, and maintain a positive work-life balance. Taking care of oneself is essential to preserving one's best mental and emotional well-being in the workplace and should not be seen as a luxury.

## Encouraging Physical Health

The foundation of general health and stress tolerance is physical well-being. This section offers helpful guidance on eating a balanced diet, drinking enough water, exercising frequently, and getting enough sleep. These behaviors support mental and emotional wellness in addition to physical health.

## Gratitude Exercises and Positive Thoughts

Developing an optimistic outlook might be a very effective stress-reduction strategy.

This chapter presents techniques such as journaling thankfulness, concentrating on strengths and accomplishments, and utilizing positive affirmations. These methods encourage optimism and assist people in approaching obstacles from a constructive standpoint.

## Using Creativity to Reduce Stress

Creative pursuits, including writing, painting, music, or crafting, offer a way to express oneself and decompress. This section encourages people to discover their creative side as a way to process feelings and feel fulfilled and accomplished.

## Outdoor and Nature-Based Activities

It has been demonstrated that spending time in nature improves mental health and lowers Stress. The advantages of spending time outside are examined in this chapter, whether hiking, gardening, or just taking strolls in scenic areas.

## Nutrition and Mindful Eating

Eating correctly is essential to general health. The significance of mindful eating—which is being in the moment and paying attention to the eating experience—is emphasized in this section. It offers advice on how to choose wholesome foods that promote mental and physical well-being.

## Using Strategies to Increase Resilience**

The capacity to overcome obstacles and setbacks is resilience. The methods for constructing resilience are covered in this chapter, including how to foster a growth attitude, learn from mistakes, and hone problem-solving abilities. These techniques enable people to respond to pressures with flexibility and confidence.

## Taking Part in Restorative Practises

It's crucial to include restorative activities in one's routine in addition to active self-care techniques. These restorative practices encourage relaxation, such as taking warm baths, doing yoga or gentle stretching, and using relaxation techniques.

## Looking for Expert Assistance and Resources

Knowing when to get professional assistance is a sign of proactive self-care and self-awareness. This chapter offers advice on how to get in touch with services like therapy, counseling, or support groups for people who might need a little more help with stress management and general well-being.

## Fostering a Culture of Health and Well-Being at the Office

Encouraging a culture of well-being at work is advantageous to the company as a whole. To improve employee well-being, companies and leaders can implement the recommendations, which include establishing flexible work schedules, providing services, and cultivating a pleasant work culture.

Individuals can efficiently manage Stress, prevent anger from building up, and enhance overall well-being by adopting these practices into their lives. This chapter highlights that to create a productive and healthy work environment, self-care is not only an individual obligation but also a team endeavor.

## <u>CONCLUSION</u>

A diverse strategy is necessary on the path to productive anger management and a peaceful work environment. Every chapter covered important topics, such as creating a productive workplace and comprehending the psychological dynamics of anger. These techniques help people better control their emotions, but they also foster an environment at work where people are respectful, empathic, and willing to communicate.

The cornerstones of handling high-pressure situations with poise and professionalism are knowing your emotional intelligence, identifying your triggers and early warning signals of rage, and using constructive conflict resolution approaches. Furthermore, putting self-care and stress management first is not just a personal duty but also a vital part of preserving mental and emotional health in the workplace.

Furthermore, companies may provide a setting where workers feel appreciated, encouraged, and inspired by cultivating a pleasant work environment. Promoting open communication, cooperation, and teamwork fosters a sense of community and group problem-solving. A culture of continual improvement is fostered by leaders who set a good example and offer chances for personal development.

In the end, this all-encompassing strategy for handling anger and improving workplace relations not only promotes individual achievement but also creates an atmosphere in which every employee may flourish. Through the adoption of these principles, organizations can foster a work environment that not only inhibits the growth of resentment but also fosters a dynamic and efficient professional community. Recall that sustained good change can only be achieved via group effort and a shared commitment to well-being is achieved.